Living in the
Country

Richard Spilsbury

www.raintreepublishers.co.uk
Visit our website to find out more information about Raintree books.

To order:
☎ Phone 0845 6044371
🖨 Fax +44 (0) 1865 312263
✉ Email myorders@raintreepublishers.co.uk

Customers from outside the UK please telephone +44 1865 312262

Raintree is an imprint of Capstone Global Library Limited, a company incorporated in England and Wales having its registered office at 7 Pilgrim Street, London, EC4V 6LB - Registered company number: 6695582

Text © Capstone Global Library Limited 2010
First published in hardback in 2010
Paperback edition first published in 2010
The moral rights of the proprietor have been asserted.

Edited by Charlotte Guillain and
  Catherine Veitch
Designed by Joanna Hinton-Malivoire
Original illustrations © Capstone Global Library
Illustrated by Mapping Specialists
Picture research by Elizabeth Alexander and Fiona Orbell
Originated by Dot Gradations Ltd
Printed in China by South China Printing
  Company Ltd

British Library Cataloguing in Publication Data
Spilsbury, Richard
Living in the country. – (Our local area)
910.9'1734-dc22
A full catalogue record for this book is available from the British Library.

Acknowledgements
We would like to thank the following for permission to reproduce photographs: We would like to thank the following for permission to reproduce photographs: Alamy pp. **10** (© Travel Ink), **14** & **15** (© Cotswolds Photo Library), **18** (© Chris Howes/Wild Places Photography), **19** (© The Photolibrary Wales), **20** & **21** (© Jeff Morgan Rural Environment); © Capstone Global Library Ltd. pp. **4**, **5**, **9**, **12** & **13** (Tudor Photography); Corbis pp. 8 (© Chinch Gryniewicz/Ecoscene), **16** (© Hulton-Deutsch Collection), **17** (© Patrick Ward); Photolibrary p. **7** (E.A. Janes/Age Fotostock); Pictures of Britain p. **6** (© Tony Rostron).

Cover photograph of Wansford-in-England, River Nene, near Peterborough, Cambridgeshire, reproduced with permission of Corbis (© Lee Frost/Robert Harding World Imagery).

We would like to thank Rachel Bowles for her invaluable help in the preparation of this book.

Every effort has been made to contact copyright holders of material reproduced in this book. Any omissions will be rectified in subsequent printings if notice is given to the publisher.

Contents

Any words appearing in the text in bold, **like this**, are explained in the glossary.

What is the countryside?

The country, or countryside, is the name for areas of **rural**, settled land outside towns and cities. The countryside is made up of natural **features** like mountains, hills, rivers, lakes, and woods. In the country you also see hedges, walls, fences, and fields that are part of farms.

Could you label the natural features, such as woods or hills, and the man-made features, such as hedges or walls, in this area of countryside?

Some areas of country have few people living there. There may be only wild animals, and animals such as sheep that can look after themselves. In many places the countryside surrounds villages and towns where people live and work.

Uplands and wetlands

In the United Kingdom there are different kinds of country. **Uplands** are areas of high ground, often **moorland** with **heather**. There are steep, rocky mountains and gently rolling hills. It is usually too cold and windy for people to live on high mountains.

Look in an **atlas** to find the nearest upland to where you live. What is the highest hill or mountain there?

Wetlands are low-lying areas of country with lots of water. There are wide lakes and **reservoirs**. There are long, twisting rivers and narrow streams. At places where rivers slow, the rivers can soak the land and form muddy **marshes**.

Do you think soft, marshy land is good land to build on?

Woods and fields

Woods are areas of country covered with trees. Some woods grow naturally and they can be very old. Leaves fall off most of the trees in autumn and grow again in spring. These are **deciduous** trees. **Plantations** are woods planted by people. **Conifer** trees are often found in plantations. They have needle-like leaves all year round.

Conifer trees are cut to make floors or squashed to make paper.

Fields are areas of country that farmers have cleared of trees in the past. Farmers grow **crops** or keep animals in fields. Some fields are surrounded by lines of trees and bushes that form hedges. Other fields are surrounded by stone walls and fences.

Stone walls in the countryside mark boundaries between land owned or cared for by different people.

Country buildings

In the countryside there are different farm buildings. You can see farmhouses people live in, barns for storing farm machines and hay, and sheds where farm animals sleep. There are also grand houses with large gardens. These were built by rich families who moved out of towns in the past.

Think of three ways in which this home is like the home you live in, and three ways in which it is different.

Country buildings	Not country buildings
farm	large school
barn	factory
stable	block of flats
country house	office buildings
church	multi-storey car park
small school	

What buildings could you add to these lists? What are the buildings like where you live?

Some people in the country live in old cottages that were built for farm workers in the past. Other people live in new houses. Some homes are next to roads near villages, but others are at the end of long tracks.

Getting around in the country

In the country there are few buses and often no train stations. Most people in the country travel by car. Many country roads are narrow and winding, so people cannot drive fast along them.

Some farmers use quad bikes to cross bumpy fields.

People can climb over **stiles** to follow footpaths across fields.

The best way to see the country is to leave the roads. Some people walk along **footpaths** to enjoy the fresh air and the peace and quiet. Some people ride horses or bikes along mountain trails or across moors.

Working in the country

In the country, some people grow crops or rear animals on farms. Other farms have changed into different businesses. They have rooms for visitors to stay in, small factories that make farm products such as jam or cheese, or farm shops.

Some farms let children visit them to feed the animals and sit on tractors.

Some people grow up in the country but have to move to towns and cities to find work. People who live in towns and cities sometimes buy houses in the country as holiday homes. They stay there mostly at weekends or during the holidays. Why do you think schools and shops sometimes close down when fewer people live in the countryside all year round?

This barn once stored hay, but people changed it into a holiday home.

In the past

In the past, most people in the country worked on farms. They grew different fruit and vegetables for people to eat in different seasons. Many **crops** were ready to pick in autumn, so farmers celebrated this time of plenty with a **harvest** festival. Today, fewer people take part in the harvest but people still celebrate the festival.

In the past there were fewer machines, so people worked together to bring in ripe crops while the weather was good.

We can find many clues about life in the country in the past. There are **ruins** of villages or buildings from long ago. Green lanes are paths that people used to travel along and move farm goods in the past.

These are the remains of a country castle. What clues are there near where you live about people's lives in the past?

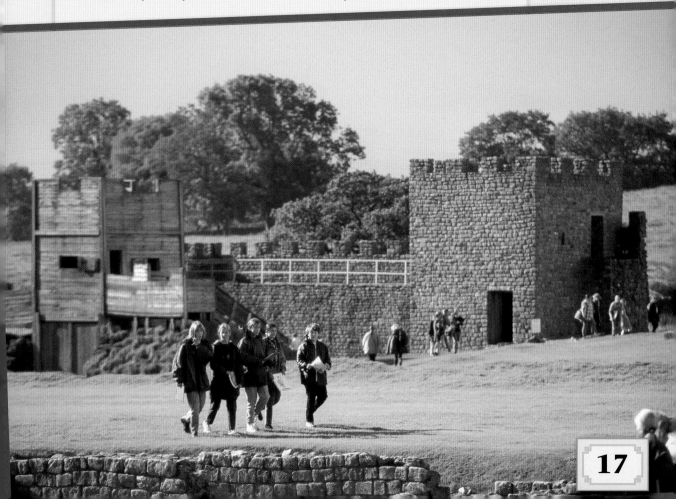

What to do in the country

Local people and visitors enjoy being outdoors in the country. They canoe on rivers, swim in lakes, and cycle on special trails through forests. They climb up mountains, run in the hills, and camp on the **moors**. They enjoy the space without too many people around.

Riding a horse is a great way to see the countryside.

All these people have come to watch bands playing music in the country.

Some people watch birds and other wildlife in the country. Other people paint pictures of the countryside. Sometimes people go to special events, such as an outdoor music festival or a horse riding show on a farm. What would you like to do in the country?

Caring for the country

Sometimes people damage the country. They wear away land on hills and mountains when they walk or cycle off **footpaths**. They leave litter or pull up wild plants. Some people even start fires in woods or on **moors** by mistake.

Many people care for the countryside. They help to mend footpaths and fences or they clear up litter. They plant wild flowers and trees for butterflies and other animals to visit for food. They also plant woods to help the **environment**. How would you care for the country?

These people are making a stone path for walkers to use so they do not wear away the land.

Finding your way

People use maps to find their way around in the country. This map shows a country area around Isley School in Dartmoor, Devon. Can you spot the school? How many parks are to the west of the school? Name three features south of the school.

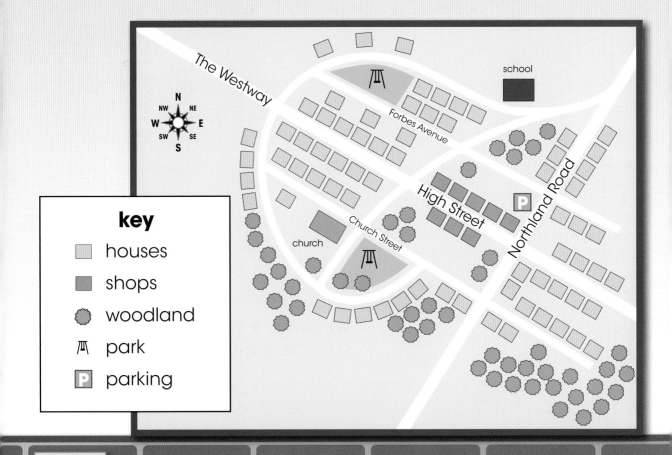

The Westway

school

Forbes Avenue

High Street

Church Street

Northland Road

church

key

☐	houses
◼	shops
⬤	woodland
⊼	park
P	parking

Glossary

atlas book containing maps and information about the world

conifer type of tree that has needle-shaped leaves and produces seeds in cones

crop plants people grow for food or for other uses

deciduous trees that lose their leaves in winter and then grow new leaves in spring

environment land, sea, animals, and plants that make up the area where we live

features characteristics or appearance of an object or person

footpath narrow path for people to walk along

harvest time of year when the crops are ripe and are gathered in

heather low-growing plant with small green leaves and small colourful flowers

marsh area of low, wet land

moor/moorland open land with peat soil and heather or bracken plants

plantation man-made forest or wood, usually where just a few types of trees are planted

reservoir man-made lake often used to store water

ruins remains of broken buildings

rural to do with life in the countryside

stile steps for climbing over a wall or fence

uplands area of high, hilly land

wetland area of wet land, such as a swamp or marsh

Index

Find out more

Books to read

Changing Countryside, Jorg Muller (Heryin, 2006)

Living in a Rural Area, Lisa Trumbauer (Pebble Books, 2005)

Websites

Ordnance Survey – Get-a-Map
www.ordnancesurvey.co.uk/oswebsite/getamap/
This site provides OS maps that can be printed or copied. Get one for the countryside near you.

The National Trust
www.nationaltrust.org.uk/main/w-index.htm
Use this website to find out about country houses, parks, and wildlife in your local area.